The Little Book of
Golf

Vic Barkes

summersdale

Summersdale Publishers Ltd
46 West Street
Chichester
West Sussex
PO19 1RP
UK

www.summersdale.com

Printed and bound in Belgium

ISBN 1 84024 388 0

In memory of Tom Edwards;
golfer, club maker and jolly good bloke

Contents

Introduction

'The game was invented a billion years ago – don't you remember?'

Old Scottish saying

There are many different schools of thought regarding the true origins of golf but it is generally agreed that the game has its roots in Scottish soil. That said, stick and ball games (that were no doubt inspirational to the ultimate sport) have been played all over the world since God was a lad. The Romans, for instance, were fans of a game that involved a ball filled with feathers, which was driven by branches fashioned into clubs. The Celts and Huns had a similar version of the game, and the Dutch used to play a type of golf on frozen canals. In China it is claimed that a form of golf was played as early as 30 BC.

But it would appear that the source of the game as we know it today dates back to medieval times. Before then golf was simply a game – and a fairly roughty-tufty one at that – in which two teams thwacked the ball about a field with the aim of driving it into a goal.

Golf grew rapidly in popularity and by 1457 it had almost replaced archery as a pastime in Scotland – a sport that was imperative to Scotland's national defence. The powers that be pulled no punches and playing golf at the expense of neglecting your arrow practice became a hanging offence. However, the brave Scots flew in the face of authority and continued to tee off on 'links' (seaside courses) – they had their priorities right!

'Playing in the U.S. Open is like tippy-toeing through hell.'

Jerry McGee

Facts from the Fairway

The first ever golf club was The
Gentlemen Golfers of Leith in 1744,
formed to promote an annual competition
with a silver golf club
as the prize.

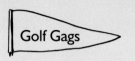

Golf Gags

Jeremy and Charles were having a pint in the clubhouse. Jeremy says:

'My wife says that she's going to leave me if I don't give up golf.'

'But that's awful!' replies Charles. *'What are you going to do?'*

Jeremy takes a large swig of beer, thoughtfully wipes the froth from his top lip, sighs, and replies:

'I'll miss her.'

Going Clubbing

The earliest types of club were pretty basic instruments, made by the players themselves, and nothing more elaborate than bits of wood fashioned into long-nosed cudgels. But as the game's popularity increased, craftsmen were employed to produce more sophisticated clubs. Such an artisan, a bow-maker from Perth, was commissioned to design and make a set of clubs for King James IV of Scotland in 1502.

Club heads were made from hard woods such as beech and holly, while ash or hazel was used for the shafts. The club and shaft were then bound together with leather. The clubs weren't especially hard-wearing and a golfer could anticipate the breakage of, on average, a club per round.

Whilst it was Scotland that became renowned for the refining and production of clubs, it was actually from the USA that the next major advancement in manufacturing came. By the 1920s hickory wood had begun to be imported and was quickly taken up as a suitable material from which to make club shafts. Further changes, improvements and experiments meant that by the 1930s there was a variety of makes of club available. To stop golfers playing with an excessive number of clubs, and in a bid to encourage skill, golf's governing body, the Royal and Ancient Golf Club of St Andrews (the R & A), introduced the 14-club rule in 1939. The system of numbering woods and irons instead of naming them was adopted thereafter.

From the end of World War II the fine-tuning of golf clubs involved more man-made materials. There is no doubt that clubs have developed enormously from the crudely carved efforts of the early game and the modern golfer has a vast choice of clubs available to them, including the lightweight graphite shaft. Trouncing steel shafts for rigidity and strength, this brilliant (if expensive) addition to the golf bag was introduced in 1973. The most popular club of all time is Callaway's Big Bertha, which hit the market in 1991.

Antique golf clubs are popular collectables. If you were to have an Allan Robertson Hickory Longnose tucked away in the attic, perchance, then you could expect to raise a four-figure sum at auction…

'We borrowed golf from Scotland
as we borrowed whiskey. Not
because it is Scottish but
because it is good.'

Horace Hutchinson

20

Facts from the Fairway

At the tender age of just 12 years,
Thuashni Selvaratnam became the
world's youngest National Champion in
April 1989. Selvaratnam took the title
after winning the Sri Lankan Ladies'
Amateur Open Championship
at Nuwara Eliya Golf Club.

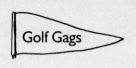

Golf Gags

Q: *Why do golfers take a spare pair of socks with them when they play a round?*

A: *In case they get a hole-in-one!*

Having a Ball

Golf balls have come a long way since the 'Feathery', one of the earliest types of golf ball. Encased in leather and stuffed, as you might expect, with feathers, the Feathery was a difficult piece of equipment to construct, and therefore expensive to manufacture. As a result, golf was known as a somewhat exclusive sport that was played only by those of significant means.

Another downside to the Feathery was that it was easily spoiled, especially in bad weather. Trying to play with a Feathery in the rain was akin to putting in treacle and golfers must have heaved a collective sigh of relief in 1848 when the 'Guttie'

came into play. Made from a substance resembling rubber which was acquired from the percha tree, the Guttie was cheaper to produce and so made the game much more accessible to the less affluent.

By the start of the twentieth century golf balls had begun to be mass-produced, thanks to industrial development and to the invention of the 'Haskell'. This ball had a rubber core, achieved by winding lengths of rubber around a thick nucleus of lead, cork or ball bearings of the appropriate proportions. It was during the refining of the Haskell that the notion of dimples on the ball was first experimented with. Dimples, it has been proved, enable a ball to travel faster and more dynamically.

The first twenty years of the twentieth century heralded the arrival of no less than two hundred differently-named balls. From then onwards much research went into the aerodynamics of the ball and in 1973 Titleist produced the icosahedron pattern, which grouped the surface of the ball into twenty identical triangles and provided a greater consistency in terms of dimple coverage.

When it comes to golf balls, size matters. The diameter of a ball must not be less than 42.67 mm nor weigh any more than 45.93 g. Balls must be spherically symmetrical and meet with various performance criteria.

A Feathery golf ball dating back to 1830 raised an astonishing £23,000 at a sale of golfing memorabilia in the UK.

'It's good sportsmanship to not pick up lost golf balls while they are still rolling.'

Mark Twain

Facts from the Fairway

Amongst the many suggestions
surrounding the origins of golf is a
charming tale. The story alleges that
whilst tending his flock in Scottish
pastures, a shepherd idly knocked a
stone into a hole in the pasture with
his crook, and thus the game
of golf was created.

Golf Gags

Jim was playing the most dreadful round of his life. Turning to his opponent, Stewart, a much more experienced golfer, he begged him for advice on how to turn his game around.

'Well, in your shoes I should shorten your clubs by about six inches,' Stewart volunteered.

'You really think that will help?' asked Jim.

'No,' replied Stewart. 'But it will undoubtedly make it easier to fit them in the dustbin.'

The Original Rules

The earliest record of the rules of the game dates back to 1744. Written for a competition set up by The Gentlemen Golfers of Leith, there were just 13 rules, which were drawn up by Duncan Forbes. The ruling body for modern day golf is the Royal & Ancient Golf Club of St Andrews.

Here are Mr Forbes's original 13 rules:

1.

You must tee your ball within
one club's length of the hole.

2.

Your tee must be on the ground.

3.

You are not to change the ball which
you strike off the tee.

4.

You are not to remove stones,
bones or any break club for the sake of playing
your ball, except on the fair
green, and that only within a
club's length of your ball.

5.

If your ball comes among water, or any
watery filth, you are at liberty to take out your
ball and bringing it behind the hazard and
teeing it, you may play it with any club and
allow your adversary a stroke for
so getting out your ball.

6.

If your balls be found anywhere touching one
another you are to lift the first
ball till you play the last.

38

7.

At holeing you are to play your ball honestly for the hole, and not to play upon your adversary's ball, not lying in your way to the hole.

8.

If you should lose your ball, by its being taken
up, or any other way, you are to
go back to the spot where you struck last
and drop another ball and allow your
adversary a stroke for the misfortune.

40

9.

No man at holeing his ball is to be allowed to mark his way to the hole with his club or anything else.

10.

If a ball be stopp'd by any person, horse or dog, or anything else, the ball so stopp'd must be played where it lyes.

42

11.

If you draw your club in order to strike
and proceed so far in the stroke as to be
bringing down your club; if then your
club shall break in any way, it is to be
accounted a stroke.

12.

He whose ball lyes farthest from
the hole is obliged to play first.

13.

Neither trench, ditch or dyke made
for the preservation of the links, nor the
Scholar's Holes or the soldier's lines shall be
accounted a hazard but the ball is to
be taken out, teed and play'd
with any iron club.

'Golf is a game in which you can claim the privileges of age and retain the playthings of childhood.'

Samuel Johnson

46

Facts from the Fairway

The Colonel Bogey March was composed by Kenneth J Alford and was inspired by golf. Whilst playing golf in Scotland he heard two notes whistled in warning further down the course. These two notes popped a tune into his head and hey presto! The Colonel Bogey March – adapted for the theme to the film *The Bridge On The River Kwai* and the jingle of ice cream vans all over the UK – was tunefully born.

Golf Gags

Q: *What do you call an enemy of Dracula who is a golf fan?*

A: *Baffy the Vampire Slayer.*

48

Tee Caddies and Handy Caps

The word 'caddie' comes from the word 'cadet' and dates back to the sixteenth century. According to history, Mary Queen of Scots, a keen player, took to using young cadets as porters; getting them to lug her clubs around the links whenever she played. 'Cadet' became abbreviated to 'caddie' and has remained in common golf parlance ever since.

Dating back to the seventeenth century, the golf handicap took its name from horse racing. Jockeys were handed their winning odds in a cap, which became known as 'hand-in-cap', latterly condensed to 'handicap'. In golf, a correct handicap makes for a more exciting match.

'Eighteen holes of match or medal play will teach you more about your foe than will eighteen years of dealing with him across a desk.'

Grantland Rice

Facts from the Fairway

Howard Hughes might have been as rich as Midas but in spite of being able to afford as many Rolexes as his heart desired, his timekeeping was still appalling. Scheduled to tee off at 1.00 pm at the Bel Air Country Club in Hollywood, he made his match by the skin of his teeth – and only because his wealth meant that he could fly himself in by private plane, which he landed on the fairway. His partner on this occasion was none other than the glamorous actress Katherine Hepburn.

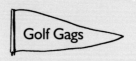

Golf Gags

Clive and his caddie are deep in the rough.

Clive: 'I say, Caddie, why do you
keep looking at your watch?'

Caddie: 'That's not my watch, Sir.
It's a compass.'

Golf on the Moon

The Apollo 14 mission of January 1971 saw Commander Alan Shepard becoming the first golfer to play a shot on the Moon. Using the handle of a geological tool Shepard missed the ball on his first shot, largely due to his cumbersome space suit, which was so bulky that he was unable to bring his arms close enough together to grip his 'club' with both hands. Two further single-handed swings proved more impressive and the balls were projected onto the lunar course. Although Alan Shepard's words at the time were *'There it goes, miles and miles and miles'*, he later corrected this and reckoned that

his two successful shots had probably travelled
200 and 400 yards respectively.

*'I know I'm getting better because
I'm hitting fewer spectators.'*

Gerald Ford

Facts from the Fairway

It is calculated that a golfer would have to play an average of 12,000 tee shots to get a hole-in-one.

BUT!

A blind lady in her seventies achieved perhaps the most amazing hole-in-one of all time on a Florida course in 1990. Even more amazing was the fact that she did exactly the same the following day at exactly the same hole!

Facts from the Fairway

Christian Carpenter, aged four years, is
the youngest golfer on record to have
achieved a hole-in-one. The talented tot
struck lucky in December 1999 at the
Mountain View Golf
Club in Hickory, North Carolina.

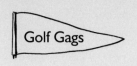

Golf Gags

Golfer: *'Caddie, do you think my game is getting better?'*

Caddie: *'Indeed, Sir. You are missing the ball much closer than you were a few weeks ago.'*

Pointers for Play

They Do It with Mirrors

One way to improve your backswing is to
stand with your back to one mirror and facing
another. Perform the action of the swing and
then use the mirrors to check the position of
your shoulders. Your front shoulder should be
beneath your chin with your back shoulder
directly in line with it. Get your stance right and
your backswing should come on
in leaps and bounds.

Gone with the Wind

To drive the ball further when playing into a
headwind, tee the ball a tad lower and from a
couple of inches further back than usual.

Gripping Stuff

A firm grip is vital to a good swing. A common error is to relax after connecting the club with the ball, when in fact the grip should be maintained and the ball swung through with careful direction towards the target.

Wet, Wet, Wet

When playing in rain or drizzle or extreme
heat, hands and clubs will get wet or sweaty,
which will render your grip less effective.
Ensure that you pack your trolley with spare
gloves, a towel and, in the heat, even
some antiperspirant spray.

66

A Good Stick

Ensuring that you are playing with the correct driver for your level of play is a fundamental way of steadying your game. Average golfers generally require drivers with lofts of around ten degrees. Beginners are likely to need a driver loft of twelve degrees. Ace players, who are better able to hit hard and fast, will need a driver loft of nine degrees or lower.

'Golf is a game whose aim it is to hit a very small ball into an even smaller hole with weapons singularly ill-designed for the purpose.'

Winston Churchill

Facts from the Fairway

Golfers have some of the most ridiculous nicknames in sport. Jack Nicklaus, for instance, is known by the handle 'Golden Bear', while Henry Picard is lumbered with the label of 'The Chocolate Soldier'. Tony Lema is known as 'Champagne Tony', Craig Stadler as 'The Walrus' and Richard Zokol, poor chap, is stuck with the more familiar title of 'Disco Dick'.

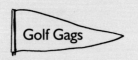

Golf Gags

Tom, Dick, Harry and Fred meet up in the clubhouse for pre-golf drinks. When they have drained their glasses Fred stays to settle the bill and the other three set out for the first tee. They are soon bragging about their sons.

Tom tells the others, 'My boy is a builder. He has been so successful that he has given his friend a new house'.

Eager to compete, Dick says: 'Ha! My lad was a car salesman but he's so smart that he now owns a chain of garages and has given his friend a brand new Ferrari.'

Not to be outdone, Harry immediately jumps in and says: 'Well, my son is an art dealer and he's done so well for himself that he's given his friend a Renoir.'

By this time Fred has caught up with them and Tom tells him that they have been talking about their sons and asks after Fred's boy.

'Well, it's good news and bad news,' says Fred. 'My son is gay and works as an escort. I'm not too chuffed about the job but he must be doing something right. His last three boyfriends gave him a house, a new Ferrari and a work of art.'

Grooves for the Green
– the golfer's top ten

1. It Don't Mean a Thing (If You Ain't Got That Swing) – Duke Ellington / Irving Mills

2. Tee for Two – Irving Caesar / Vincent Youmans

3. The Birdie Song – The Tweets

4. Sultans of Swing – Dire Straits

5. I Get A Round – The Beach Boys

73

6. Eagle – Abba

7. Queen of Clubs – KC & the Sunshine Band

8. Hot Shot – Barry Blue

9. Drive On – Brother Beyond

10. Albatross – Fleetwood Mac

Golfing Horoscopes

Aries

As the boldest risk-taker of the zodiac, adverse
weather conditions will seldom put Arians off
playing a round. However, their fiery tempers
make them the most likely star sign to be
reprimanded by club officials for the use of bad
language and for bloodying a fellow golfer's
nose. Irritatingly, they are usually very good
players and win more games
than they lose.

Taurus

Taureans are slow-but-sure players. Easygoing most of the time, they are rarely troubled by pre-game nerves and are good conversationalists between holes. They are sensual people and this often shows in their swing when their hips take on the most seductive 'jiggle'. Taureans are organised and determined characters, which makes them ideal candidates for the post of social secretary. Your club raffles will be legendary.

Gemini

Easily bored and thoroughly two-faced, Geminis will change clubs and partners at the drop of a hat. They are highly competitive and very talkative characters, and can't resist telling everyone how to play each shot. They will also drive other players mad by having protracted conversations on their mobile phones during a round. Whilst their competitive nature generally makes them fairly good players, their moods swing as often as their clubs. First to the bar, they are last to produce the readies and get their round in.

Cancer

Soft-hearted they may be in day-to-day life, but on the golf course Cancerians are real fighters. They are known to have a keen eye and, generally, good physique. However, their tendency to sidle up to other players and give them a sly pinch before they play an important shot does them no favours when it comes to being included in a round of drinks in the clubhouse.

Leo

The most dramatic and extravagant of the golfing signs, Leo's equipment will always be the most expensive and the most exclusive. Leo will wear the loudest trousers and sweaters. The laziest and greediest sign of the zodiac, their caddies will buckle beneath the weight of energy drinks and chocolate bars, as well as a video camera so that Leo can be filmed showing off in a disgustingly OTT manner. Playing golf is an event of theatrical proportions to lions and they expect lots of applause for any half-decent shot.

Virgo

Most likely to customise their own clubs, which will always be meticulously cleaned after each round. They are often nominated as the club First Aider and can also be seen donning the chef's hat at the annual summer barbecue. Always good for the loan of a tenner when you have forgotten to go to the cashpoint and it's your turn to get the gin and tonics in.

Libra

Caring, sharing and utterly charming, Librans always manage to resolve any conflict between other players. Famed for their perfect balance, they are the most likely players to win a game played in high winds. Very into nature, there are more Librans that play nude golf than any other sign.

Scorpio

The sexiest sign of all and blessed with an
extremely fertile imagination, Scorpions will flirt
madly with other players of the opposite sex,
even if it means compromising their game.
They often have a terminally ugly caddie in tow
as this better enhances their own physical
charms. Will invent wild and ridiculous reasons
as to why they miss easy shots.

Sagittarius

Sagi is the eternal optimist of the zodiac. Their glass is always half full and they believe that they will win every game that they play. They have an appealing, childlike curiosity, but this often lands them in hot water when they get caught red-handed delving into fellow players' golf bags to 'see what they are made out of'.

Capricorn

Forceful, charismatic and mischievous, Capricorns are sticklers for rules and traditions but always have a 'twinkle' about them. Very astute at seeing through people, it is almost impossible to pull the wool over their eyes. However, their Achilles heel is their zest for adventure, which nearly always results in them getting disoriented, tattered and injured during a game. Oh, and losing, too.

Aquarius

Sociable but eccentric Aquarians will always stand out in a golfing crowd, usually by wearing completely the wrong sporting outfit. Aquarians will be chatty with fellow players, but may scare would-be friends off with their talk of the course being invaded by obese, five-toed killer badgers.

Pisces

The most generous player of the zodiac, Pisces will not only turn a blind eye to minor cheating but will also sign up for all the dull committees that no one else will touch with a bargepole. Very creative and artistic, they are the sign most likely to indulge in recreational drugs.

And finally…

*Golfing tales that encompass the weird, the
wonderful and the damn silly*

Naked Golf

In 1966 there were several naked golfing incidents in Macomb County's Washington Township. It appeared that some residents were very partial to a round played in the buff, which wasn't the least bit popular with some of the more strait-laced members of the community. The 'Committee to stop Topless Golf Outings' was duly formed and a local ban on public nudity was swiftly put in place.

Cow-in-one

The 18th hole at St Margaret's-at-Cliffe Golf
Club in the UK was the scene of a terrible
tragedy in 1934. A cow died instantly when the
club's pro hit poor Daisy with his tee shot.

Heavy Metal

It is alleged that in 1912 a gentleman by the name of Harry Dearth played a match at Bushey Hall, England clad in a full suit of armour. Under the somewhat weighty circumstances it is no real surprise that he lost.

Gull Cull

The 1935 Society of One Armed
Golfers' Championship boasts an
extraordinary double-whammy.
J. Perret managed to fell and kill a seagull
with his first approach shot. Incredibly, he
did the same to another bird with his
second approach shot.

A Lump in the Throat

A golf club in Germany was in deep trouble in
1994 when a farmer filed a lawsuit against the
club's owners for the murder of no less than 30
of his cows. Evidently a vet had investigated the
death of the cows and had found a golf ball
lodged firmly in the throat of one of the late
heifers. Closer inspection proved that all 30
had swallowed golf balls – a staggering 2,000
in all – which had been hit from the course
into the neighbouring pasture.

Holiday Haul

Customs officials smelled more than just a rat when talking to a supposed tourist who claimed he was on a golfing holiday. Whilst making idle chit-chat about the sport the officials realised that the man had no grasp of even the most basic terms of the game. Upon being asked to demonstrate his swing the 'tourist' did so – backwards! A search of his luggage revealed large quantities of narcotics, which were carefully stashed in his golf bag.

Well and Truly Shafted

Back in 1951, Edward Harrison was enjoying a day's golf at the Inglewood Country Club in Seattle. His pleasure was seriously thwarted when, without warning, the shaft of his driver broke and punctured his groin. One can only guess at the agony he experienced before he finally collapsed and escaped to the great fairway in the sky.

www.summersdale.com